From Tragedy to Triumph

My Paducah Experience

DEAN SIKES

Pathway
PRESS

Book Editor: Wanda Griffith
Editorial Assistant: Tammy Hatfield
Copy Editors: Cresta Shawver
Oreeda Burnette
Esther Metaxas
Inside Layout: Mark Shuler

ISBN: 0-87148-348-3
Copyright © 2000 by Pathway Press
Cleveland, Tennessee 37311
All Rights Reserved
Printed in the United States of America

Dedication

To my wife,

Lori,

I have not yet discovered words that
adequately describe the depth of my love for you.
It seems that every day I discover something new about
you, something that uniquely makes you who you
are. Your continued and unwavering commitment
to our marriage, our family and our foundation
is a gift from God that comes second
only to eternal salvation.

Table of Contents

Acknowledgments

MY FAMILY

To *Lori*, my wife, thanks for being with me on this journey we call The Spirit of America. I love you with all my heart.

To my father-in-law, *Bill Turner*. Thanks for teaching me the difference between expectation and expectancy. Your initial edit of this manuscript helped me dig a little deeper and search more passionately for the key ingredient that must come to the surface for each of us to migrate from tragedy to triumph.

THE PATHWAY PUBLISHING FAMILY

Thanks for believing in my message and in this book. Thanks especially to *Dr. Dan Boling* and *Dr. Bill George*. When you agreed to publish this book, you helped our outreach transition to the next level of service to people who come from all walks of life. I look forward to seeing what the Lord has for us, as together we offer people, young and old alike, that intangible asset of hope.

There are two other people from the Pathway organization to whom I owe a heartfelt thanks—*Wanda Griffith* and *Wayne Slocumb*.

Wanda is the book editor at Pathway. Thanks, Wanda, for your straightforward, yet sensitive input and suggestions that took this book to a higher level of excellence. I am so thankful to God for placing you in such a strategic position. I am equally thankful that I listened to your counsel.

Wayne is the graphic arts manager at Pathway. Early in our relationship, Wayne and I had a couple of conversations about what I envisioned for the cover of this book. I will never forget sitting in his office watching as the Lord directed Wayne through the creative process that gave birth to what I believe is the cover design God himself desired for my book. Truly, Wayne, your gift has made room for you.

Our Staff

Saying thanks seems so inadequate, but oftentimes, less is better. Because you do what you do, I am enabled to do what God has called me to do; for this, I say thanks.

Thanks to our board of directors for always being available to listen and offer godly counsel. The cumulative amount of wisdom that is embodied in our board is something I do not take lightly; indeed, through the years, I have learned to lean on you as together we rely upon Him.

Our Longtime Friends and Consultants

Don and Judy Provine are special friends. Whether we're in a strategic planning meeting around my conference table or in one of our all-day marathon sessions at your farm, or maybe you've joined us on the road to see some of the fruit of your labor, one thing remains consistent—your heart for our outreach to encourage, motivate and inspire teenagers to become all they were created to become has never wavered nor diminished. Even though I never see all you do for us behind-the-scenes, God does, and He keeps excellent records.

To *Mark Jacobus*, a creative genius. From our very first conversations, I saw in you a hunger to help young people discover their respective futures. I am so thankful that you find time to help me help so many. I'm glad you're on the heavenly team, and I am watching, with a great expectancy, to see your gifts used to further enhance the lives of a generation of teenagers.

My Pastors

Alan and Terri Crider, you're much more than our pastors—you're family. Because of your position, you see what no one else sees and you hear what no one else hears. Through it all, somehow you maintain your focus, and you consistently feed our family the uncompromised Word of God. Sadly, many people in today's society never learn to depend upon their pastor. In what we do, Lori and I not only depend upon you and your gifts, we can't imagine our lives without your input, guidance and support. We love you.

Introduction

On December 1, 1997, when I heard the news that there had been a school shooting in a small town in western Kentucky, I was immediately drawn to the people involved—especially the students.

As the reports from the media shot across the airwaves, and some of the worst fears relating to possible student deaths were confirmed, I remember having a deep-seated compassion for so many people whose lives would never be the same—all because of the horrific actions of one young man.

Sitting in the den with my wife that December evening, I vividly remember a divinely inspired thought scrolling across the marquee of my heart: *One day, Dean, you will go to Paducah and be given the opportunity to share your heart with many of those involved with this event.*

Little did I know that within 19 months I would be invited to bring my message of hope and encouragement, purpose and value to the very campus I was observing on television.

Of the books I have written thus far, this one is the most exceptional to me personally. It holds this distinction for one reason: Through my visit to the campus of Heath High School, I met with students, faculty and staff who had the courage to stand against evil, to rebuild a dynamic school community. By doing so, they offer hope to each of us that we too can go *From Tragedy to Triumph.*

Chapter One

THE TRAGEDY

With this headline on December 1, 1997, word circulated throughout the nation and the world that the unthinkable had occurred in West Paducah, Kentucky: "Student Kills Three, Wounds Five at Kentucky School."

At 7 a.m. on December 1, 1997, few people outside the small, rural town of West Paducah, Kentucky, had ever heard of Heath High School. Fewer still had heard of a 14-year-old freshman named Michael Carneal. By 2 p.m. that same day, not only had we learned of Paducah, but the events at Heath High School were also thrust front and center onto the world stage.

FORCES OF GOOD AND EVIL

On that cold December morning in Kentucky, forces of good and evil were at work. At 7:30 a.m., as they did every morning prior to school officially starting, around 35 students came together in the front lobby at Heath High School to pray. As the students stood in a circle holding hands, singing songs and praying to God, a young man stood alone, unnoticed by anyone. This young man's actions would forever change lives not only at Heath High School, but also lives around the globe.

That morning, by all accounts, Michael Carneal, a student at Heath, came to school with a devilish mission and an arsenal to carry out his plan. He also brought with him five guns, four of which were wrapped in tape in a blanket. He brought over 1,200 rounds of ammunition—1,200 rounds of firepower for a school that only had 600 students enrolled.

Sound of Gunfire

As the group brought their prayer meeting to a close, the young man calmly put ear plugs in his ears and reportedly pulled out a .22-caliber Luger handgun. He then assumed a firing position and pulled the trigger. As the bullets fired, students fell. The first bullet hit a popular 14-year-old freshman. With bullets spewing through the air, an ever-increasing number of students fell to the ground.

Hearing the unmistakable sound of gunfire, Mr. Bill Bond, principal at Heath High School, made his way out of his school office and into the hallway—literally putting himself in the line of fire.

Front of Heath High School

As the shots rang out, Ben Strong, the leader of the prayer group, yelled, "Mike, what are you doing? Put the gun down!" Michael ignored the voice of Ben Strong and continued his deadly assault.

In the horror and confusion that followed, it was reported that Michael began reloading his weapon. At that moment, Mr. Bond moved into the open space of the school hallway and looked into the eyes of Michael Carneal. As suddenly as the horror had begun, it was over.

Putting the gun down onto the bloody floor tiles, Michael reportedly looked at Ben Strong and flatly said, "I can't believe I did that."

THE AFTERMATH

Eleven shots had been fired, eight students were struck. In all, three students were killed, and five others wounded. Those who died as a result of the shooting were Jessica James, a 17-year-old student who was active in both her school and community; Nicole Hadley, a 14-year-old freshman who was on the girls' basketball team and a member of the school band; and Kayce Steger, who was also in the Heath High School band and was engaged to be married.

Often when I speak, I share with audiences that *it is always darkest just before the light.* As a speaker who invests enormous amounts of time and energy into the lives of teenagers from all walks of life, I frequently encounter people who experience and *come through* dark moments in their personal lives. Never before, however, have I had the honor of investing some of my time with people who have come through a darker time than those at Heath High School . . . people who have exhibited in the truest form of the words: courage, tenacity and forgiveness.

By design, the first portion of this book is short. I chose not to dwell on all that has been written about the events of December 1, 1997. Instead I have chosen to invite you to join me on a journey—a journey that began with tragedy, but ends in triumph.

Chapter Two

THE CALL

As I landed in Atlanta, the temperature was in the 90s. I walked off the plane, across the tarmac and into the hustle and bustle of Atlanta's Hartsfield International Airport. Arriving at the connecting gate, I checked in with the agent, received my boarding pass, and walked over to a bank of payphones. I dialed my voice mail number to retrieve any messages that may have arrived since I began my trip to Florida for a speaking engagement at a weekend convention.

HOLDING TO GOD'S PROMISE

As I listened to one message in particular, I almost shouted right there in the middle of Concourse B. The voice of the messenger was a young, but mature high school freshman who was offering me an opportunity that would change my life and the life of our foundation.

Several weeks prior to my receiving this message, while in prayer the Lord spoke ever so gently to my heart, telling me that He would send me into every high school that had experienced a shooting. This news both humbled and inspired me. It humbled me because of the circumstances I would be experiencing; it inspired me because of the possibility that I would soon have the opportunity to speak where few others have spoken.

The one ingredient God did not reveal to me was *when* He was going to send me to these schools. He just gave me confident assurance that it would happen. Having a history of walking with God, I know that He is faithful and that He never lies. I took Him at His word and began to believe Him for the manifestation of what He had whispered to me during prayer—*one day I would speak at high schools that have had shootings.*

For weeks prior to this Friday morning phone call, I had been praying and believing that at the appointed time, I would see doors open I could never open on my own. One Bible verse in particular was becoming wonderfully familiar to me: "I know your deeds. Behold, I have put before you an open door which no one can shut" (Revelation 3:8). Because of the enormous amount of publicity and media exposure the school had received, I knew it would be next to impossible for my office to schedule me to speak at Heath. But I also knew that if I believed God, I would have what He told me.

Dean Sikes and Pam Wrinkle

FAITH UNLOCKS THE DOOR

From personal experience and from what I have seen in the lives of others, I know that faith is the key that unlocks the doors of opportunity for me to bring my message of hope and encouragement, purpose and value to students who have survived school shootings.

So when the phone call came from that student at Heath, I immediately knew in my heart this was the first school, the first *open door* I would walk through as a direct result of what I had heard in prayer.

After talking with the student and Heath's guidance counselor, we confirmed the date. Then I boarded the plane and was off to speak in Florida. By all accounts and every measurable standard, the event in Florida was tremendously successful. Flying home, I nestled in my seat to pray and think through some decisions. One decision in particular weighed heavy on my heart.

By the time I landed in Tennessee, I had peace about my decision not to share with too many people the news that I was going to Paducah. The Bible says, "Even a fool, when he keeps silent, is considered wise" (Proverbs 17:28).

It wasn't that I was not excited about the opportunity to speak with the students at Heath High School. On the contrary, that was precisely the reason I chose to keep the event in a non-publicized category. Let me share with you my thinking.

THE GOLDEN RULE

As I dissected all of the emotions the students, faculty and staff at Heath must have endured since the tragedy, I attempted to place myself in their position. Identifying how I would appreciate being treated if the roles had been reversed, brought me to the decision of not undertaking a promotional campaign. Doing so would align me with those who have attempted to receive promotional gain from what clearly was a tragic event. My decision to refuse a self-promoting campaign became one of the wisest choices I made relating to my Paducah experience. Here's why.

Chapter Three

THE SCHOOL

o you know the old saying, "Time flies"? Sure enough, the days leading up to my appointment at Heath truly flew by. Days quickly turned into weeks, and suddenly, it was time for us to begin our trip to Paducah.

As my wife, Lori, and I traveled ahead of our staff and a couple of our friends who were joining us later that evening in Kentucky, I phoned the school and spoke with Pam Wrinkle. Pam was instrumental in developing the "Rising to the Challenge" program I was only hours away from kicking off in a morning assembly.

As Pam and I talked, I asked her if she would be opposed to contacting the local newspaper in Paducah in hopes of securing an interview for me after the assembly program. I surmised that any exposure I received *after* speaking at Heath could do no harm to the school and would be a blessing to our foundation.

GOD: THE PROMOTER

Pam immediately responded with an answer that caught me so off guard I actually found myself laughing aloud. Pam and I concluded our conversation, said our goodbyes and hung up. I looked over at Lori and said, "You're not going to believe this. Not only is the Paducah newspaper covering our event, but local and regional television stations are also coming, and *The Today Show* is already on site awaiting an interview with me and others who comprise the 'Rising to the Challenge Program' at Heath High School."

As we drove up the Kentucky interstate with farmland on both sides of the highway, Lori and I smiled at each other. Again, we had seen evidence that God is the single most creative and effective promoter in the universe. God's Word reminds us, "Cease striving and know that I am God" (Psalm 46:10).

After checking into our hotel, Lori and I visited for a moment with the friendly clerk at the front desk and asked her to please recommend a restaurant for dinner. She suggested one of her personal favorites, assuring us that we would be pleased.

After arriving from Tennessee only half an hour earlier,

the last thing we wanted to do was ride one more mile in a car. Lori suggested we walk to dinner instead. Walking hand-in-hand, neither of us knew what to expect the next morning. All we knew for sure was that God had sent us to this school, and He had a special plan for our time in Paducah.

Dean Sikes and Bill Bond, principal

Dinner was enjoyable. What seemed like only minutes, was actually almost two hours. We laughed, we talked about our kids, and as I reached for a dinner roll, I knocked my water glass across the table—causing more laughter. All in all, our dinner date was a blast, but with my wife, even the simple things we do together are special—for no other reason than we are together.

A STEP INTO FEAR

As Lori and I began our walk back to the hotel, we took an alternate route. Strolling through what appeared to be a revitalized section of a riverfront development, we walked alongside one of the most peaceful rivers I have ever seen. As we sat on a table beside the bank of the river, I took an introspective look into my heart, genuinely wondering what God wanted me to say to those at Heath High School who had come through an event that changed their lives forever.

Frankly, I was becoming anxious, allowing the pressure of speaking at such a high-profile event get to me, and I did not enjoy what I was feeling. In a sentence, I stepped out of faith and stepped into fear because *I* took control of the mission at hand.

TRUSTING GOD

My life and the life of our organization are based on a sure foundation of faith. As a speaker, I rely 100 percent on my faith in God and in His faithfulness to His Word and to me. You see, in all my years of speaking, I have never read a speech to an audience. In fact, to be perfectly honest, I never know exactly what I am going to say.

Please do not misunderstand what I am sharing with you. Before speaking, I pray, and do what I know to do to get ready for the event. I believe God knows who is in the audience, and He knows what each member of that audience needs to hear. So years ago, I took God at His word. I told Him if He would give me the opportunity to help teenagers discover their purpose and value, I would go wherever He sent me and say whatever He put on my heart. I trust God, and I trust that if I have done my part, He will do His part. And you know what . . . He always has and He always will.

Chapter Four

THE PEACE

By design, I am an organized person. I like to
know what's going to happen, and even more
importantly, I like to know when I should
expect the desired results. Little did I realize it while
sitting on that picnic table beside the river, that God
was letting me experience and work through all of
these emotions. I am convinced that He was allowing me to come to the end of myself. In His wisdom,
God was gently reminding me that it was He who had
brought me to this point, and it would be He who
would navigate me through what I believe to be the
most important time of ministry thus far in the life of
our foundation.

If I could offer some simple, yet perhaps profound,
advice right here, it would be this: No matter how far
you go in this life, never stop doing that which brought
you success in the early days. If you and I are faithful

in the little things, God will give us the opportunity to be faithful in greater areas of service.

LEAVING THE RESULTS TO GOD

Sitting with Lori on the table, watching the sun set and feeling the breeze from the water, I came to the humbling realization that on my own, I could not successfully accomplish the purpose God had established for this trip and outreach. I needed His guidance, direction and presence. Just as quickly as I had taken the control, I eagerly gave it back to God and left the results to Him. The moment I gave Him back the reins of my life and my upcoming time at Heath High School, the apprehension and concern I was feeling departed, and peace from heaven pervaded my heart.

The next morning came early. Unable to sleep, I quietly got out of bed and walked outside on the porch that overlooked the river. As I stood there praying and gathering my thoughts for the assembly, I realized it must be what science defines as the darkest point in the night. Within minutes of stepping outside in the darkness of the early morning, without warning, as if a global light switch had been activated, I watched the sun rise on the eastern horizon. Truly it can be said that it is always darkest just before the light!

A few minutes later, Lori joined me on the porch, and together we watched as a new day in Paducah, Kentucky, began to take shape.

Dean Sikes

I am convinced that every day each of us is given the opportunity to make a difference in the lives of others. As we dressed and made our way to the front desk of the hotel to check out, I knew in my heart that I was prepared. My opportunity to make a difference was quickly approaching. In Ecclesiastes we read, "There is an appointed time for everything. And there is a time for every event under heaven" (3:1).

As we drove away from the hotel, out of town and into the countryside of West Paducah, my mind traveled back to the time in prayer when God had told me He was going to send me to this very school.

TRUSTING GOD'S WORD

"God is not a man, that He should lie" (Numbers 23:19). When He says something, you can take it to the bank. His Word is faithful, alive, powerful and sharper than any two-edged sword. I relived the times in prayer when I fervently believed that this day would come.

FIRST GLIMPSE OF HEATH

I smiled as I recalled the voice-mail message that served as a point of initial contact between Heath High School and the Spirit of America Foundation. Crossing over a set of railroad tracks, we drove around a corner and suddenly caught our first glimpse of Heath High School.

This was the day and the time that God had orchestrated for me to share my heart with the students and staff of Heath. Before getting out of the vehicle, I took one last moment to gather my thoughts, say a quick prayer and receive a reassuring smile from my most trusted adviser—my wife, Lori.

As I closed my door and walked across the street, every step I took carried me closer to a moment in time for which God had created and called me. "And as for you, you meant evil against me, but God meant it for good in order to bring about this present result" (Genesis 50:20).

The front lobby of the school was alive with the hustle and bustle that accompanies the first day of a new school year. I walked around groups of young people who showed little interest in the increasing number of television crews moving about the halls.

I made my way down the corridor toward the holding room filled with teachers, local officials and volunteers. Everyone had purposed in their hearts to make this first day of school a smashing success. I grinned as I watched scores upon scores of teenagers walking, talking, smiling and still others laughing—genuinely enjoying each other's fellowship.

Standing Still

The first bell of the day rang. As students scurried off to their homeroom classes, I found myself being drawn back down the long corridor toward the front lobby of the school. When I arrived at the perimeter of the lobby, I could not help but notice that I was by myself, just me and the memories of what had happened in this very location on the morning of December 1, 1997. I was alone in the quietness and peaceful serenity of the lobby.

For the first time since receiving the invitation to come to Heath, the reality of my surroundings came flooding to the forefront of my heart. I stood in that lobby where an assault of evil had been launched. My thoughts raced to the individuals involved in the event that had brought me to this school. I didn't know what to do next, so I did what the Bible says to do—when you've done all you know to do, stand (see Ephesians 6:13, 14). So, I stood still.

GOD'S MISSION

As I stood for a moment longer alongside the memorial to Jessica, Nicole and Kayce, the peace of God flooded my soul as I remembered: What the devil meant for harm, God will turn into good (see Genesis 50:20). Sure enough, in the quietness of that lobby, I was beginning to understand God's mission for me that was now only moments away.

Chapter Five

The Assembly

T he noise of a school bell is like none other. Once the bell rang, my moment of silence came to an abrupt halt as students emptied out of classrooms and entered the hallway from every direction. I walked back into the holding room where I met several more local dignitaries. After a few moments of exchanging pleasant conversation, Pam Wrinkle told me that it was time to go to the auditorium.

Listening

Taking Lori's hand, we walked toward the school auditorium that by now was filling up with teenagers. Unnoticed by the students, I made my way to one corner of the auditorium and began an exercise I routinely undertake before speaking with any audience: I watch the people. God has given me two eyes, two ears and one mouth. My translation of His creation?

When we listen and watch twice as much as we talk, we become more effective communicators!

Standing off to the side, I was approached by *The Today Show* reporter and sound engineer. After they wired me for sound, I returned to my corner of the auditorium to watch, listen, and most importantly, to pray.

TIME TO INSPIRE

I never enter into an event with a personal agenda. I choose instead to speak *with* the audience instead of *to* the audience. Preparing for this assembly was no different than the preparations I have done for hundreds of other events. It was no different except for the fact that this time, the audience was comprised of teenagers whose school was known for an act of violence that left students injured and, in three instances, dead.

To say that the circumstances that brought me to Heath High School did not pass through the reasoning portion of my brain would be misleading and wrong—they did. I chose, however, not to spend my time on stage focusing on a tragedy that had occurred at the end of 1997. Instead I made the decision to invest my time inspiring the students at Heath to learn from the past, to plan for the future and to maximize their potential every day.

How, though, could I not even mention the shootings? How could I let the students know that those who were suffering from the gunshots and indeed those who had lost their lives were not forgotten? So much has been written about the three ladies who lost their lives, but what about the other young victims who had become living testaments of the will to live? What could I say that had not already been said before?

HIDING THE WORD

Again, I was letting the pressure come back to me. Again, God reminded me that He was with me and would be with me when I spoke. This time the Word hidden in my heart was manifested at the perfect time. It was one I have stood upon for years as a speaker: "Do not become anxious about how or what you should speak . . . or what you should say; for the Holy Spirit will teach you in that very hour what you ought to say" (Luke 12:11, 12). And you know what? He did exactly what His Word said He would do! "The desire of the righteous will be granted" (Proverbs 10:24).

After calling the assembly to order, welcoming the students to a new school year and giving me a gracious introduction, I heard the words, "Please welcome to Heath High School Dean Sikes from the Spirit of America Foundation." And with that, I found myself briskly walking up four steps, shaking the hand of the assistant principal, grabbing the microphone and greeting over 650 people.

Students at Heath High School (Missy sitting)

Walking back and forth across the stage, my eyes darted across the audience, adjusting to TV lights and flashing cameras. At first I was nervous. And then, as I settled down and saw the students at Heath as just that—teenagers who were excited about their respective futures and life in general, I felt the peace of God. Only then could I thoroughly enjoy my interaction with the students during the assembly.

POWER OF BELIEVING

I spoke at length about how each of us can reach our true potential, touching on the importance of coming to terms with previous hurts and disappointments. However, I felt led to invest the majority of my time talking about the power of believing.

Maybe you're sitting in this audience today and you have a pretty good idea of what you want to do with your life; but like me, maybe you too see no one in your world who is successfully accomplishing that dream you know to be uniquely yours. Because you see no one fulfilling this niche, perhaps it's also difficult to believe what you want to do can actually be accomplished. If I'm describing what you're feeling, have I got some exciting news for you today! Let me explain.

Back in 1992, I had a dream to travel our nation and other nations of the world where I would meet teenagers from all walks of life and, through my speaking and products, offer them the hope that their individual lives have a godly purpose and an eternal value. I knew that nothing in life ever becomes dynamic until it first becomes specific, and so I set out on a journey to craft a specific plan of action that would soon give life to my dream.

Throughout this process, I kept looking at others who were speaking with teenagers, and you know what? I could not identify any speaker who was saying what I wanted to say. I actually began to question the validity of my message to see if there was a place for my message. As I prayed about this slight onset of confusion, the Lord gently spoke to my heart and told me that it was not my job to compare myself to any other speaker. It was my job, my responsibility, to believe that not only was I called to reach young people, but that He had also created a niche for me and for my message. Again, my job was to believe.

As I worked through this process, I discovered what was to become a liberating truth: *Maybe I saw no one saying what I wanted to say to teenagers because I was the one person on the earth God had chosen to communicate, in my own unique way, this message of hope and encouragement and personal purpose and value; maybe I knew of no one who was doing what I wanted to do because I was the one person who was supposed to be doing it.*

Now here's a liberating thought for you: If you can relate to what I have just said, then maybe, just maybe, it's time for you to stop wondering and choose instead to begin believing! Want a radical thought to help jumpstart you on this journey? Think about that dream you want to accomplish. Think about the amount of time, energy and resources that will be needed for you to be successful. Count the costs of what you will have to personally expend in order to accomplish your dream.

Now, see yourself at your weakest moment—that moment when you actually want to quit. When everyone around you says that it can't be done, that no one in your family has ever gone as far as you are proposing to go, that you are a fool for even trying. At that moment, look deep in your heart and ask yourself two questions: (1) If not me, then who? and (2) If not now, then when?

You were not created by accident. Your life has a definitive purpose and value. I dare you to become all you were created to be.

Near the close of my presentation, I shared an encounter I had years ago in central Florida with a young man who gave birth to the central theme of my message. Here's what happened.

FLORIDA ENCOUNTER

It was a hot and humid August morning in Florida as the sun rose. When I arrived at the high school, I met the principal and participated in a brief sound check. I then settled in a chair on the front row of the theater where, in only a matter of minutes, hundreds of teenagers would come pouring into the assemblies from four separate entrances.

After being introduced, I delivered my opening remarks and began to talk about each of us having value and a purpose. I asked a rhetorical question and began to watch the reaction on faces throughout the audience. Some of the

From Tragedy to Triumph

students started squirming, while others thoughtfully considered my question. Some snickered, and some chose not to make eye contact with me, fearing that I would call upon them to give an answer in front of their peers.

LOOK AT ME!

Near the back of the auditorium, I made eye contact with one young man. It would have been next to impossible not to see him; he wanted to be seen, and he wanted to become involved in the dialogue.

As I acknowledged him, I repeated my question, "How many here know what you would like to do with your life . . . what's your dream?" I asked this student named Fred, and his response caught me somewhat off guard. He said, "I want to become a drug addict."

Everyone laughed, and immediately Fred became the center of attention. I asked a couple of others what their dreams and ambitions were. Suddenly, I saw Fred's hand once again excitedly waving in the back of the school theater.

I thought for a second and then made the decision to call on Fred again. I remember asking him if he had a *serious* dream he wanted to share with us. He assured me that this time he was going to be straight. I took the bait and repeated my initial question.

With an earnest look on his face, Fred blurted out, "I want to go to prison." This time, the laughs from his peers were sporadic, and Fred realized that perhaps he should have stopped after his first answer. As I brought the assembly to a close, I invited students to come down to the front of the stage where we would have the opportunity to talk. Responding to my invitation, students flooded the stage area.

Chapter Six

THE WALLS

As I was talking with students in central Florida and listening to their responses, I watched for Fred. Would he have the courage to make his way down to the stage and discuss his answers? As I continued meeting people, I looked up, and coming down a long walkway toward the stage was Fred. I was delighted.

TURN AND RUN

Suddenly, Fred became aware that I had noticed him. He stopped abruptly only a few feet away from scores of his peers who were sharing their views on my presentation. Fred had a decision to make. Would he continue toward me, or would he turn and walk out of the theater?

The internal pressure he was feeling must have been

intense, because in a split second, Fred turned and briskly walked toward the exit. I now had a choice to make: Should I stay and talk with and listen to all of the students who had received what I had said, or should I politely excuse myself and go after the *one* who desperately needed to know that his life had purpose and value? *Should I stay or should I go?* became the question of the day.

Dean Sikes

As I quickly thought through my options, I was reminded of the Biblical story of a Shepherd who was watching 100 sheep on the side of a hill. One of those sheep wandered away from the flock, placing the Shepherd in the valley of decision—a valley that proved to be similar to my own situation. The Shepherd, knowing the value of each of the sheep in His care, chose to leave 99 and go after the one. Why? I believe the Shepherd understood that every life counts—that each of our lives has value and a purpose. I reached my decision.

CHASING ONE SHEEP

Politely excusing myself from the large gathering of students, I promised to return in five or 10 minutes, and followed Fred out of the auditorium. Looking over his shoulder, Fred appeared to be surprised that I was behind him. He walked a little faster, I walked faster; he began to jog, I jogged. He then appeared to lose some of his composure and began to run as fast as he could; I was just a little faster.

As I caught up with him, Fred was taking long, deep breaths. I looked him squarely in the eyes and asked him two simple questions: "Have you ever used or experimented with drugs? Have you ever been to a prison?"

Fred's short response was, "No."

What do you think Fred was looking for during the assembly? I believe he was desperately searching for something he apparently was not receiving anywhere else—he wanted some attention. In my thinking, he needed someone to *believe* in him.

BREAKING DOWN THE WALLS

As Fred and I talked, the walls began to come down. With each passing moment, Fred and I began to connect at the heart level. I was not in Florida to judge him; I was there to offer him and others what I call *the intangible asset of hope*. As we continued our conversation, I felt that inner prompting to say four simple words. With a genuincness that moved Fred to tears, I looked him in the eyes and pointedly said, "I believe in you."

DREAMING OUT LOUD

Clearly, Fred had never had these words spoken to him, and he wasn't sure how to respond. After a moment he asked me how I could believe in him, since I didn't even know him. I had never met him and certainly didn't know him well enough to make that statement. That's a fair question, I thought. So I told him why I believed in him.

I began by saying to Fred that he was created by God—he wasn't put on this earth by mistake. Because he was breathing, it was my sincere belief that there was something wonderful for him to accomplish with and through his life. I asked him to seriously think about who he was and what he wanted to become. I asked him to think big—really big—to dream out loud and share with me his greatest desires.

I went on to explain that he should pursue what he wanted to do in life, even if he didn't see anyone else pursuing what he wanted to accomplish. Maybe he was the one person God put on this earth to go after and successfully accomplish the dreams that were residing in his heart. In other words, if not Fred, then who; and if not now, when?

NEWNESS IN LIFE

At that moment, perhaps for the first time in his 17 years, Fred caught a glimpse of a clean canvas upon which he was being encouraged to paint the dreams, ambitions, goals and objectives that would frame his future. As Fred and I stood in the courtyard of his central Florida high school, he began to dream. He began to stretch his imagination and see himself in a new light. He was slowly cutting the chains of yesterday's pain and disappointment to embrace newness in his life.

This clean canvas Fred discovered was the same clean canvas I was inviting the students at Heath High School to envision and then to embrace. With the doors to the auditorium open and a large-blade fan pulling the hot August air of western Kentucky into the auditorium, I took one last look at the students, faculty and staff at Heath High School. This was one of those moments in my life that I simply did not want to end. I was sensing many varied emotions, but the single greatest emotion was gratitude to God for having been given the opportunity to do what I am called to do with teenagers.

THE ASSET OF HOPE

My message to teenagers is what I call "the intangible asset of hope." On this day, the students at Heath, through their response to my message, offered hope to me.

As I brought the assembly to a close, I did so by saying, "Learn from your past, plan for your future, and live today to its maximum potential. I believe in you. God bless you."

With that, the assembly ended. Sustained applause filled the auditorium. As I stood there smiling back at so many happy expressions, the verse came to me again: "The desire of the righteous will be granted" (Proverbs 10:24).

WHAT ABOUT THE SHOOTING?

As I walked off the stage, I was met by reporters and cameras. One reporter in particular wasted no time in voicing her concern: "You had these students in the palm of your hand," she began. "If you had asked them, these kids would have gotten up and followed you out of this auditorium. Having their attention the way you did, please explain to me why you never mentioned what brought you here in the first place. Why did you never mention the shooting?"

My response to this reporter was that the shooting at Heath High School was in the past. There was no reason to drag this school community back into the pain and sorrow that had placed this school on the front pages of newspapers across the United States.

A Gift Called "Today"

I believe some of the most God-inspired counsel I offer young people who attend our events is the same counsel I shared with those who gathered for the assembly at Heath High School: Refuse to let your past rob you of your future. Yesterday is forever gone. The Bible assures us that we have no guarantee of tomorrow, but we have been given a gift called "today." People who choose to live in the mistakes, heartaches and disappointments of yesterday miss out on the blessings of today.

My point to this reporter is the same point I want to impart to you. Refuse to be governed by and harnessed with tragedies from your past. Make the choice to look deep within the confines of your heart and believe that you have the heart of a champion. Champions never quit, they do not live off yesterday's tragedies nor triumphs—they keep their eyes fixed on the prize.

Walking away from me, the reporter seemed to be pensively reviewing our brief encounter. My hope and prayer for her and for you is that you will live each day with a passion no tragedy can ever diminish.

As I mentioned earlier, when the assembly was over, the verse that came to my heart was, "The desire of the righteous will be granted." Little did I know that when my conversation with this reporter came to an end, the most meaningful moment of my trip to Paducah for me personally was quickly approaching.

Because my speaking schedule keeps me moving from school to school, I often have to leave one school soon after I'm off stage to ensure that we are on time for our next scheduled event. Because of our limited amount of time at each location, years ago I wrote a book that serves as our follow-up program for students who hear our message. Our foundation freely gives kids from all walks of life their personal copy of this book.

MEETING MISSY

As the students at Heath filed out of the auditorium, many of whom graciously stopped to express their personal appreciation for my assembly, I watched with such thankfulness as every student at Heath was given a copy of my book.

As the last students made their way back to their individual classrooms, I walked over to a couple of teachers and listened as they shared with me their positive reaction to my assembly. Then I found myself asking a question that I would have only felt comfortable asking a teacher or perhaps Mr. Bond, the principal. I wondered if anyone at my assembly had been at the school when the tragedy had occurred. One of the teachers responded that many students today were at Heath on December 1, 1997. In fact, three of the students who had been shot had just heard me speak. One student, Missy, in particular grabbed my attention. Lori and I asked to meet her.

FORGIVENESS IN ACTION

Moments later, seated in a wheelchair with a smile

that brightened up the hallway, Missy made her way down the slope of the hallway, shook my hand and introduced herself to Lori and me. The three of us talked for a while, and Missy seemed genuinely touched by what she had heard me say. What Lori and I noticed most about Missy was the love of God that clearly and powerfully radiated her personality. She exhibited no bitterness for where she was in life. Never once during our conversation did she even hint of having a pity party or bring up the inevitable question many in her position may have asked, "Why me?"

Missy shared with Lori and me some of her plans for the immediate future. We discussed the possibilities of Missy and I speaking together at assemblies and church youth events at some point in the future.

Chapter Seven

THE TRIUMPH

In my research for this book, I was shown an article published in *Today's Christian Woman* magazine. One quote from this article attracted my attention because it is my belief that what I discovered while reading this feature is the reason Missy is not a bitter person. The quote that grabbed me? "I need to forgive him." *Forgiveness*—a big word with even bigger ramifications. Here's a portion of the article:

> But is she bitter about what happened—especially toward the guy who pulled the trigger? "It's weird," Missy said, "but you know, I don't have any bad feelings toward him—no revenge thoughts or anything like that. I felt like I needed to forgive him." That's just what she told Michael's family when they visited Missy in the hospital soon after the shooting. "I just told them that I wasn't upset at them, and I'm not upset at Michael."

FROM PAIN TO VICTORY

The very definition of the word *tragedy* carries with

it the idea of pain, discomfort and sadness. Likewise, the meaning of *triumph* centers on victory. How do we then migrate from pain to victory? Forgiveness. No matter who you are, no matter where you live or the circumstances in your past, the path from tragedy to triumph is brightly lit by a willful decision to forgive those who caused you pain and sadness.

Of all the teenagers I have met in life, Missy certainly can be counted among those who chose to display the determined resolve to become all she was created to be. Truly, she has within her the heart of a champion. Like multitudes before her, and multitudes to follow, it is my belief that Missy discovered this heart of a champion when she chose to forgive.

MOMENTOUS ENCOUNTER

There is a verse in Proverbs that says, "A man's gift makes room for him, and brings him before great men" (18:16).

I choose to believe the Bible—every single word of it. And so, the gift God has given me has indeed made room for me, and has again and again brought me before some great men and women. The people I have had the honor of meeting, people whom our society would quickly decree as *great,* include one U.S. president, several vice presidents, numerous members of Congress, business and industry leaders, entrepreneurial giants both in the United States and abroad, sports heroes, and spiritual leaders of faith. I add to this impressive list of encounters a group of students and faculty of Heath High School in a small town in Kentucky.

Monument to slain

After our time with Missy came to a close, Lori and I rejoined our staff and friends and headed back to the holding room for some refreshments. As we walked, a member of the school staff stopped me to tell me several television stations were ready for interviews. I excused myself and began to make my way toward the reporters. Meeting the reporters and cameramen, I found myself immediately and deliberately listening to the still, small voice that will speak to anyone who has ears to hear.

A Light to the World

With each interview, I was mindful of the power of the media. I knew that I might be given only one opportunity to get my message across. I was determined to make the most of each opportunity. With every question, I made it my goal to not only answer the question, but to go a step further—to praise the efforts of the people at Heath who chose to press on into what I believe will be their most promising and exciting days as a school community.

With all the media attention spotlighting Heath, it was obvious that this school was being given the opportunity to *let their light shine* and, by so doing, become a light to the world. "You are the light of the world" (Matthew 5:14).

As my time at Heath came to a close that day and I said good-bye to so many people who had become our friends, I did so with mixed emotions. The predominant stirring within me was one of thankfulness to God for having given me the opportunity to speak and minister at Heath High School.

Never the Same

Walking back toward our vehicle, Lori and I stopped

in front of the school's main entrance and silently looked at the memorial marker that is adjacent to the school's front door. I knew then that our lives would never be the same, and I was passionate about our future.

Driving away from Heath High School, I took one final glance in my rearview mirror. I saw the bright sunshine atop the building where earlier the forces of good and evil had battled. As the school disappeared from my view, I knew in my heart that the people at Heath had come from tragedy to triumph.